I WAS THERE

VIKINGS

I WAS THERE
VIKINGS

JOHN D. CLARE

Consultant Editor DOMINIC TWEDDLE

RIVERSWIFT
LONDON

First published in Great Britain in 1991 and reprinted 1994 by The Bodley Head Children's Books. This edition published 1994 by Riverswift, Random House, 20 Vauxhall Bridge Road, London SW1V 2SA.

Random House Australia (Pty) Ltd
20 Alfred Street, Sydney, NSW 2061, Australia

Random House New Zealand Ltd
18 Poland Road, Glenfield, Auckland 10, New Zealand

Random House South Africa (Pty) Ltd
PO Box 337, Bergvlei 2012, South Africa

Copyright © 1991 Random House UK Limited
Text copyright © 1994 John D. Clare
Photographs copyright © 1991 Charles Best

John D. Clare and Charles Best have asserted their right to be identified respectively as author and photographer of this work.

ISBN 1 898304 62 9

A CIP catalogue record for this book is available from the British Library.

Photography Charles Best
Director Tymn Lintell
Production Manager, Photography Fiona Nicholson
Designer Dalia Hartman
Visualization/Systems Operator Antony Parks
Editor Gilly Abrahams
Editorial Assistant Valerie Tongue
Map Simon Ray-Hills
Time-line John Laing
Typesetting Sue Estermann

Reproduction F.E. Burman Ltd, Columbia Offset Ltd, Dalim Computer Graphic Systems U.K. Ltd, J. Film Process Ltd, Scantrans, Trademasters Ltd.

Printed and bound in China

ACKNOWLEDGEMENTS
Make-up: Alex Cawdron, Sarah Packham.
Model-makers: Chris Lovell, Neville Smith.
Old Norse language adviser: Dr Richard Perkins.
Picture research: Valerie Tongue.
Props: Mark Roberts.
Set design and building: Art FX Associates.
Set dresser: Jennifer Nevill.
Viking co-ordinator: Phil Bertham.

Random House would also like to thank the following: Andrew Jones of The Archaeological Resource Centre, York; Pete Butler; Jeff Clarke; the Henson family, Cotswold Farm Park; Peter Gardner and Linda James, Cultural Resource Management, York; Mike Haywood; Jomsborg Elag Dark Age Re-enactment Society with the assistance of the Norse Film and Pageant Society, London; Lehrer Viking Museum, Denmark; Colin Levick; Pete Pienot; The Rare Breeds Survival Trust Ltd; Kim Siddorn and Roland Williamson of Regia Anglorum; Colin 'Rab' Richards; Rosguilda Ship Museum, Denmark; Square Sail Ship-yard, Bristol; York Archaeological Trust and The Jorvik Centre, York.

Additional photographs: Julian Bajzert, pp1-5; Icelandic Photo and Press Service, pp32-3; Spectrum Colour Library, pp8-9; Swedish Tourist Board, pp30-1; Werner Foreman Archive: p6 bottom right (Thfodminjasafn, Iceland), 46-7, 63 (Statens Historiska, Sweden); Zefa Picture Library, pp12-13, 40-1.

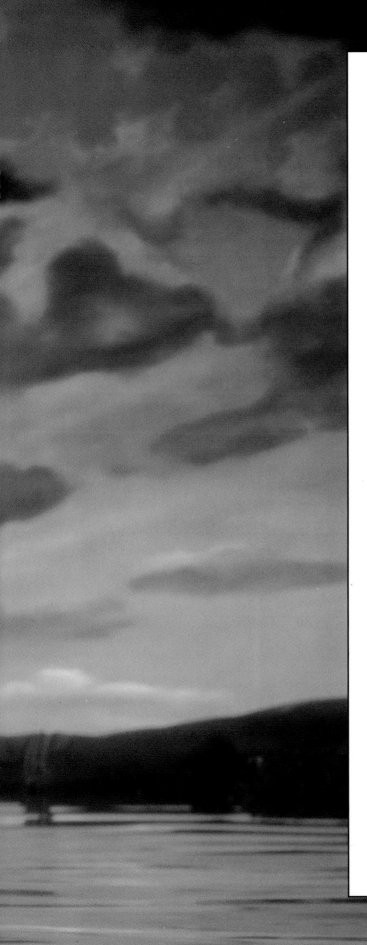

Contents

The Vikings Are Coming!

The people who lived in Scandinavia from about AD 800 to around 1100 are known as the Vikings.

The Old Norse word *víkingr* meant pirate, and many people think of the Vikings only as fierce raiders. The Vikings, however, were also remarkable explorers, conquerors, settlers, traders and craftsmen. They developed just laws and a system of democracy.

The Viking world

Although the same language (Old Norse) was spoken all over Scandinavia, the Vikings were never one nation. At the beginning of the Viking age their first loyalty was to their clan (a group of related families) and there were many different regions, each with its own ruler. Gradually, during Viking times, the three kingdoms which make up modern Scandinavia – Norway, Sweden and Denmark – were formed.

By contrast, in AD 800 the rest of Europe was dominated by three powerful empires. The Holy Roman Empire included France, Italy and Germany, and was ruled by the Emperor Charlemagne. In the East the city of Byzantium (present-day Istanbul) was the centre of the wealthy Byzantine Empire. To the south and east of the Mediterranean Sea lay the Muslim Arab Empire.

The Vikings had no central government or co-ordinated policy, yet for three hundred years they were able to terrorize these three great empires.

Religion and sacrifice

The Viking gods were fierce and merciless. Odin, the god of war, ruled over Valhalla, the Hall of the Chosen. He rode across the skies on an eight-legged horse, accompanied by wolves. Warriors who died in battle were taken to Valhalla by the Valkyries (warrior maidens). In this Viking heaven they fought all day and feasted all night. Odin was also the god of wisdom and the father of writing and poetry. You could not really trust Odin.

Thor, the god of thunder, was the most popular of the gods. Ordinary people wore lucky charms made in the shape of the hammer that he carried. Thor supported

law and justice, which is why the Icelandic Assembly (the Althing) always opened on a Thursday (Thor's day).

Frey, the god of harvest, and his sister Freyja, the goddess of love, ensured good crops and large families. Their father, Njord, was the god of wealth, fishing and sailing.

Both Odin and Frey required sacrifice – on infrequent occasions, human sacrifice. Captured enemies were spread-eagled. A cut was made down the spine, the rib-cage was opened sideways and the lungs pulled out like an eagle's wings.

An eleventh-century German writer, Adam of Bremen, was told by a Christian of a festival at Uppsala, in Sweden, which was held every ninth year and lasted nine days. If his informant was telling the truth, nine males of several kinds of creature, including man, were slaughtered and hung up on a sacred tree by the *gothis* (priests). They dipped birch twigs in the blood and sprinkled it over the worshippers. The Vikings believed that Frey was most pleased by the sacrifice of horses; for this reason Christians of the time were forbidden to eat horsemeat.

The greatest sacrifice was to give a son. When war against neighbouring Vikings was going badly, Hakon, ruler of Norway (965-95), promised to sacrifice his young son, Erling. Matters improved immediately and Hakon gave the boy to his servant to be put to death.

powerful enough to declare war on the Holy Roman Empire. Although he was unable to defeat Charlemagne, he destroyed the trading town of Reric and persuaded its merchants to move to a new town he had built in Denmark. Its name was Hedeby. Godfred was not a mindless killer. He was using Viking military and naval power to develop trade and increase his country's wealth.

There followed three centuries of Viking raids, travel and conquest.

In the beginning

In spite of their religious rituals, the Vikings were not uncivilized barbarians. In the eighth century their Scandinavian ancestors already had a form of democracy and extensive trade links. On the island of Helgö, near Stockholm, archaeologists have even found a bronze Buddha from India.

Treasure troves of coins and jewellery have been discovered which show that Sweden, in particular, was very wealthy. They also show that the century before AD 800 was a time of warfare in Scandinavia – the treasure had been buried by owners who did not survive to collect it. During this period the Vikings developed their fighting spirit and pirate tactics, becoming skilled sailors and navigators. Travel and raiding became part of the Scandinavian way of life.

Nobody really knows what inspired the Vikings to attack the rest of Europe, but by AD 808 Godfred, King of Denmark, felt

Viking Homelands

There were three classes of people in Viking society. The *jarls* (earls) were the chieftains and military leaders. At the bottom of society were the thralls (slaves). In between were the *bóndis* (freemen) whose land was *óthal* (it belonged to them).

A wealthy freeman or freewoman would own a *bær* (farmstead) and about 30 thralls. Slaves could be identified by their closely cropped hair and their white coats. They did the digging, sowing and harvesting – although a hard-working slave might be promoted to *bryti* (farm steward) or *deigja* (housekeeper). They belonged to their master who was allowed by law to beat them to death, providing he publicly announced what he had done on the same day. Some farmers let their slaves work for money or share in the profits of raids. In this way they could earn enough money to buy their freedom.

On small farms the whole family had to help in the fields and look after the animals. In one saga (story) a young Viking named Grettir was put in charge of the geese (he killed them) and the horse (he skinned its back so it never wanted to go outside). Quarrelsome and aggressive, Grettir was the ideal Viking son – the kind of boy whose exploits would be remembered in the sagas.

The main building of the *bær* is the low wooden longhouse. Sometimes farmers cover their roofs with tar or turf to make them more waterproof. In summer children play on the roof and goats have to be discouraged from climbing up to eat the straw. Other buildings include a byre (cow house), barns, stables and a bath-house.

The best place for a *bær*, the Vikings believe, is at the foot of the high grassy slopes. In summer the farmer grazes his livestock on the mountain pastures. Wealthy farmers move with their families and slaves to a shieling (summer-house) in the hills.

Inside the Longhouse

Archaeologists have excavated a Viking long-house at Stöng in Iceland. The main hall was about 40 feet (12 metres) long. There was also a day room for the women, a food storage room, and a room which might have been a cold store. Along each side of the hall there were banks of earth, which served as seats by day and as sleeping places at night.

Viking halls did not have glass windows, but sometimes in the gable end there was a small *skjár* (opening). A *skjall* (the membrane which covers a new-born calf) was stretched over it. Almost transparent, it let in just enough light 'so that men indoors can recognize each other'. In many halls, however, the only light came from the flickering fire.

The fire was built on a large, clay-covered hearthstone. If a baby was born deformed or was thought to be death-fated (unlucky), it was left out in the open to die. Sometimes the thrall was told to kill the child and bury the body under the hearth.

In the roof was the *ljóri* (smoke hole) which was also a useful escape route if an enemy set fire to the house.

A Viking wife runs the household. The thralls help her do the everyday jobs – cooking, spinning and weaving – and are disciplined if they misbehave. The woman of the house is also in charge of the keys to the chests which contain the family valuables. When her husband leaves to go raiding, he publicly hands over his keys as a sign that she is now in charge of both the house and the farm.

Cleaning, however, is not an important part of housekeeping, so the floor is covered with rubbish.

Winter Activities

In Viking times the climate in Scandinavia was warmer than it is today. Winters, nevertheless, were harsh, so the farmer and his family left the shieling and returned to the *bær*. They made the winter sacrifice (14 October) to ask the gods for mild weather. On 12 January they held the Yule sacrifice. It lasted three days, during which time the *gothis* sacrificed a 'forgiveness boar' and asked Frey, the fertility god, for prosperity and peace.

For the Viking men winter was largely a time for leisure. They repaired their tools and weapons. According to a Viking poet, the sons of *jarls* and freemen learned to 'shoot arrows, ride on horseback, hunt with hounds, brandish swords and do feats of swimming' – skills they would need when they went to war. Adults' pastimes included wrestling, a ball game called *knattleikr*, and juggling with knives. Men challenged each other to climb up a sheer rock face or jump off a cliff. In this way they maintained their fitness and readiness for battle.

Violence was a part of everything the Vikings did. They enjoyed watching stallions fight until one killed the other. In swimming competitions contestants tried to drown their opponents. Wrestling and *knattleikr* often ended in death. Even *hnefatafl*, a board game, could end in an argument and a blow which set the blood flowing.

Clockwise, from bottom left: the Vikings play board games such as merils (similar to draughts) and *hnefatafl* (the board and pieces resemble those used for chess, but the rules are different).

The women make braids and decorative edgings for clothes, using their skill at tablet-weaving, while the children play with dolls, go skating wearing bone ice-skates, and play a bat and ball game nicknamed 'kingy bats'.

Games that prepare the players for battle occupy much of the Vikings' time. Boys practise swordplay using wooden swords, and their fathers wrestle to increase their strength.

Shipbuilding

In April, when winter was over, a victory sacrifice was made to ask for success in the summer raids, then the men began to build or repair their boats.

The Vikings loved their boats. They gave them names such as *Raven of the Wind* and *Ocean-striding Bison*. Decorations, such as gold-plated dragons and carvings, were added. When a Viking longship set out, the women came down to the water's edge and

proudly watched the warriors row away. It was every boy's dream to captain a Viking ship.

There were many different kinds of ships, including fishing boats, cargo vessels and warships. The longest warships measured 180 feet (55 metres). *The Long Serpent*, which belonged to King Olaf Tryggvason of Norway, measured 120 feet (37 metres). A ship discovered at Gokstad in Norway was 76 feet (23 metres) long.

To their enemies, Viking ships were terrifying. Their prows were often carved to look like dragon heads; the sails represented their

wings and the oars their legs. Sometimes, however, the prow was left plain or carved in the shape of a man or bison.

Below: the base of this Viking ship has been built, and the internal supports are being added. At the prow and the stern the crossbeams are tied on with leather thongs to give the ship flexibility.

The lower strakes (side-planks) are only 1 inch (2.5 centimetres) thick. They overlap and moss or animal hair covered in tar is clamped between them to make the ship watertight.

Tools used by Viking shipwrights include an axe (far left) for trimming the strakes, an adze (above left) for shaping curves, and a moulding iron (above) for planing wood.

A Viking Raid

In Europe during Viking times events were recorded by priests and monks. The raid on Lindisfarne in AD 793, for example, was described by a twelfth-century English monk called Simeon of Durham. He tells us that the Vikings trampled on the altar and seized the precious ornaments, and that the monks were kidnapped, put to the sword and drowned in the sea.

In his account the Vikings seem blood-thirsty and invincible. He stresses their barbarity because he hated them – they had attacked an English monastery.

The Saga of the Men of Orkney on the other hand, written by a Viking, describes the raids in a very different way. Svein, a *jarl*, helps to sow and harvest the crops on his farm in Scandinavia, but in spring and autumn he goes on successful raids. In this account the Vikings seem generous and brave.

Viking raiders believed that they were fair fighters. Their laws forbade them to attack traders, farmers or women. Nor were they allowed to attack a man who was already involved in a fight.

The Vikings had their own peculiar idea of honour. The great Icelandic hero Egil Skallagrimsson was the perfect Viking – 'thick-necked, powerfully built and taller than any man.' Once, taken prisoner by a peasant, Egil stole the man's silver and escaped. As he ran, he realized that he was behaving like a thief, so he returned and killed the peasant. Then he carried away the treasure with a clear conscience.

Speed is the key element of a Viking raid and the longships are perfectly designed for sudden attacks. The warriors sail up onto the beach, carry out the raid, load the ship with captives and booty, then escape before a defence can be organized.

17

Battle for the Raven

A French monk wrote that after AD 800 Norwegian and Danish raiders 'carried everywhere the fury of fire and sword, gave up the people to death and captivity, devastated all the monasteries and left them filled with terror'.

In fact the Vikings were often defeated but each year they returned. Gradually they began to settle on the Orkney and Shetland Islands to the north of Scotland, making slaves of the inhabitants. They built forts in

Ireland and used them as bases from which they attacked the Irish monasteries. In 844 the Vikings established themselves on islands off western France. In 850 the Viking raiders overwintered in England for the first time.

The raids had become an invasion. In 865 a number of Viking *jarls* joined together to form a great host (army) which for the next 30 years terrorized western Europe. Northern and eastern England were conquered and became the Danelaw. On 6 January 878 the Danes surprised the English king, Alfred, and overran Wessex in the south of England.

Alfred and a small guerrilla band hid in the marshes. After a series of battles they forced the host to surrender. The Danish leader and his men were baptized as Christians and settled in East Anglia.

It is January 878. Facing the English, the Vikings form a shield wall. They fly their raven banner, which they believe will bring them victory.

After the first charge the battle becomes a free-for-all. This time the raven fails the Vikings: hundreds of men are killed and the famous banner is captured.

Inset left: Viking soldiers take up a pig's snout formation to defend a narrow gap.

Tribute and Danegeld

In 880 some of the Vikings left England to ravage northern France and Belgium. In 886 they even made an unsuccessful attack on Paris, already a thriving town. The Viking host also invaded Germany, then crossed back into England.

In many areas people paid a tribute, to bribe the Vikings to go away. During the ninth century the French alone handed over a total of 685 pounds (311 kilograms) of gold and 43,042 pounds (19,524 kilograms) of silver. In 911 King Charles of France gave part of his kingdom to a Viking called Rollo the Fat in return for his promise that he would drive away the other Vikings. Later on, this area was called Normandy, because the 'north men' lived there.

In 980 the attacks started again. The Vikings demanded more and more money as tribute from the English. These payments were called the Danegeld. In 1012 the Danes demanded 48,000 pounds (21,772 kilograms) of silver plus a ransom for the Archbishop of Canterbury. When they were not given the extra money they pelted the archbishop to death with bones and cattle heads.

Four years later Cnut of Denmark conquered England and took a Danegeld of 82,500 pounds (37,422 kilograms) of silver, which he used to pay off most of his army. In Sweden alone archaeologists have discovered over 30,000 early English coins – more than have been found in England.

Monks and a young landowner ensure the safety of their district by paying tribute to the Vikings.

Weapons and Warriors

The most feared Vikings were the berserkers – warriors who fought furiously in battle. It is thought that they chewed fly agaric, a poisonous toadstool, and that this caused a kind of hypnotic rage. When the berserkers were battle-crazed in this way they believed that neither sword nor fire could harm them. Before a battle they would grind their teeth and bite the edges of their shields. Sometimes, if the fury came upon them while they feasted, they would rush out to wrestle with boulders until the frenzy wore off.

Although berserkers were respected in Viking society, they were dangerous. A writer of the time described them as 'not bad people to talk to as long as you don't upset them'.

The Vikings, such as this warrior (top centre), Rus trader (centre) and bowman (below right), treasure their weapons and battle garments, giving them poetic names. A byrnie (below) might be called Odin's Shirt.

Right, top to bottom: a helmet (which does not have horns and might be called War Boar); small daggers; a spear and an axe (Wolf of the Wound); bow and arrows (an arrow might be named The Glad Flyer); and two swords (which might be called Odin's Flame or Viper of the Enemy). The best swords, imported from Germany, are inlaid with the signature of Ulfberht the blacksmith – one of the first brand names.

Viking arrows have specially designed flights (above, far right) and heads (bottom centre) for every task from killing men to catching fish.

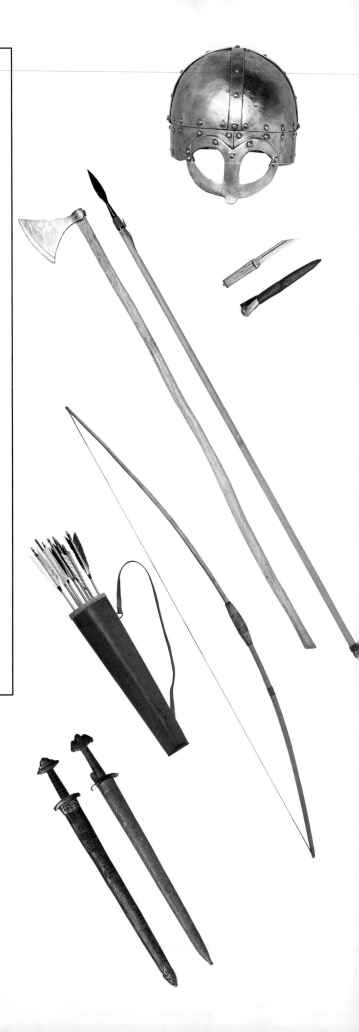

Raising an Army

When the king needed to raise an army he sent a messenger round the country with an iron arrow. Norway and Denmark were divided into *skipreitha* (ship districts), each with its own thegn (war leader). Every man who saw the arrow, including thralls, had to join the war leader's ship within five days, combed, washed and fed, or be outlawed. Even widows had to send their men servants.

In theory, therefore, a Viking army was made up of troops of levies (men who had been called up), each led by a thegn or *gothi*.

The warriors of the great raiding armies, however, were probably professional soldiers, recruited in the towns. It is hard to believe that ordinary Viking farmers would be asked to spend up to 30 years away from home. These Viking warriors fought for a share of the treasures they captured. After a battle the spoils were carried to a pole in the middle of the battlefield and divided between them according to rank.

Below: crews vary in number depending on the size of the ship, but usually there are about 30 men. Each rowing place is called a room and the size of a ship is measured by the number of its rooms. The warriors sit on chests, in which they store their weapons and clothes.

Right: levies bring equipment for the voyage, including weapons, a cauldron, sacks of grain, water barrels and drinking horns.

Left: a rich Viking brings a byrnie and other personal possessions such as a drinking horn, a comb, fire-lighting equipment and dice made from antlers. He inspects an arrow to see if it is straight.

Burial Ceremonies

The Vikings mourned their dead. In *Egil's Saga*, when his son died Egil shut himself in his room and refused to eat. His daughter joined him. She was eating seaweed. 'Is it harmful?' asked Egil. 'Very,' she replied. 'Do you want some?'

When a Viking warrior died, the ceremony of *nábjargir* was performed. First his eyes and mouth were carefully closed and his nostrils sealed. Then an old woman known as the angel of death washed the dead man's hands and face, combed his hair and dressed him in his best clothes.

Viking funeral ceremonies varied from place to place. In some areas a dead man or woman would be buried in a mound, but in others the body was cut up and taken to different parts of the country. In Russia, where many Vikings settled, the body of a chieftain would be placed on a ship which was set on fire by the dead person's nearest relative.

Most people were buried with all the things that they would need in the afterlife, including beer and food, weapons, jewellery, clothing, horses and dogs – sometimes even a peacock. Rich women were buried with their cooking equipment and embroidery work.

A slave girl has agreed to be buried with her master. In imitation of a Viking marriage ceremony she drinks and celebrates, then goes on board the ship (see inset, left) to lie down beside the dead man. She believes she will be the warrior's consort in Valhalla.

While the men beat a rhythm on their shields, the slave girl is strangled and the 'angel of death' thrusts a dagger into her heart.

Feasting and Storytelling

Next to fighting, feasting was the Vikings' favourite occupation.

On the day of the feast the woman of the house ordered her servants to set out the tables and put embroidered hangings on the walls. Straw was spread on the floor and the *skapkers* (beer barrels) were brought in. Then servants were sent to invite the guests, who were expected to wear their best clothes for the occasion.

It was a great honour to be asked to sit next to the host, although sometimes the guests drew lots to decide where they would sit. If a young man continually drew a place next to the same girl, he was expected to marry her.

A Viking host had to provide the best food he could afford. Meat was usually spit-roasted or boiled, but sometimes the men simply

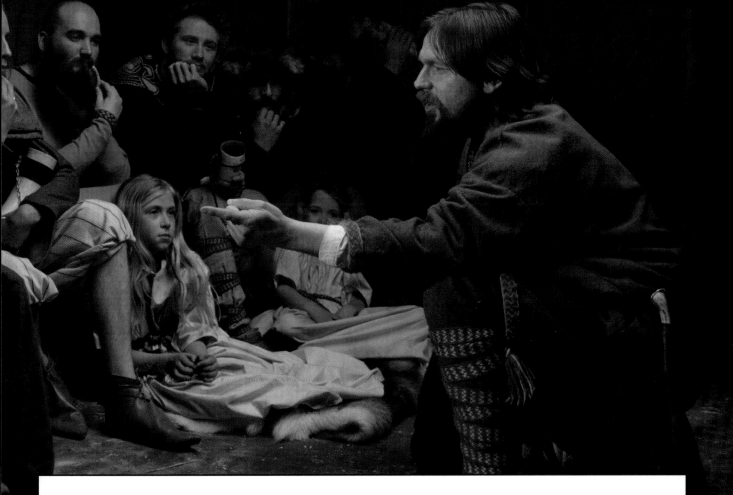

warmed the meat inside their shirts, then ate it raw. A great deal of fish was eaten – raw, dried, pickled, smoked or salted. Sausages were made from lard, blood and meat. The food was seasoned with garlic, mustard and horse-radish, and sometimes with spices brought by traders from the East.

The host's daughters, helped by the thralls, served ale and imported wine to the guests. Viking drinking horns could not be set down when filled, so they had to be emptied all at once. Drunkenness was common; sometimes a hall would be attacked by rival warriors when the men were too drunk to realize what was happening.

Poetry and storytelling are two of the _íthróttir_ (skills) that are especially valued in Viking society. At the feast the host sits in his rightful place between the decorated high-seat pillars while the _skáld_ (poet) tells one of the stories of Odin.

Stories of the gods and the great heroes are passed down from generation to generation by word of mouth.

Writing in Runes

Rune-writing was the most important of all the *íthróttir* (skills). Runes were the letters of the Viking alphabet, which was called the *futhark*. The name came from its first six letters: *f, u, th, a, r* and *k*. The Vikings did

ᚠᚢᚦᚨᚱᚲ ᚺᚾᛁᚨ ᛋᛏᛒᛘᛚᛉ
f u th a r k : h n i a s : t b m l R

not write on paper. They carved the runes on wood and stone, so the letters of the *futhark* consisted of straight lines.

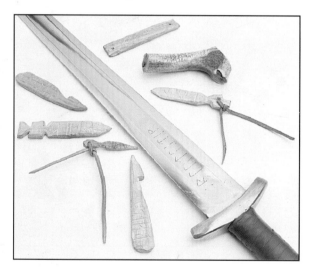

Wherever they went the Vikings left rune graffiti on rocks and buildings. 'These runes were carved by the man most skilled in runes in the western ocean,' boasted one of a group of Vikings who were sheltering inside an ancient burial mound on the Orkney Islands. 'Lif, the earl's cook, carved these runes,' a woman wrote. 'Ingigerth is the most beautiful of women,' declared another Viking. He was being sarcastic. Next to his message he drew a picture of a drooling dog.

The Vikings believed that runes had magical qualities. A man who knew the runes

could blunt his enemies' weapons, break his chains and make a woman fall in love with him. Runes would cure his illnesses, protect him in battle or at sea and guard him against witches.

Rune stones were decorated with intricate patterns and black, red, blue and white paint. They were erected to establish the right of an heir to an inheritance, or to record the achievements of those who, for example, 'journeyed far for gold' or 'shared out the spoils of war in Frisia'. Some stones record misdeeds – for instance, 'Höskuld lied to his oath-sworn friend'. Others are memorials to loved ones: 'Birging, rest in peace, loved by me, Vag.'

Although there are many runic alphabets, the Danish version (top left) is the most common.

Centre left: runes might be inscribed on a sword blade to give magic powers, or carved on small bone or wooden markers to prove, for instance, the ownership of a sack of grain.

Above: a craftsman carves the phrase 'and Holmfrid' on a memorial to a Viking woman.

Right: the Lingsberg rune stone in Sweden is a memorial to Halvdan, an eleventh-century Viking. The cross at the top of the stone shows that he was a Christian, but the carvings of dragons and other beasts reflect pre-Christian beliefs.

Voyagers to Iceland

The Vikings discovered Iceland in about AD 860 and in 874 two Norwegian brothers set out to colonize the island. With them, according to the sagas, went 3,400 settlers. Although most of them were Scandinavian, some were Irish slaves.

The emigrants sailed in cargo ships called *knörrs*. They brought the high-seat pillars from their longhouses, animals, seed, looms for making cloth, whetstones to sharpen knives and bellows for the forge. Below deck were the implements they would not be able to make until their colony was established: axes, spades, swords, cooking cauldrons and mouldboards for ploughs.

Sea voyages were hazardous. No-one knows exactly how the Vikings navigated, but three hundred years later the instructions given to sailors were no more scientific than this: 'Sail south of the Faroes so that the sea seems to be half way up the mountains.' The Vikings steered with a large oar called a steerboard on the right-hand side of the ship, which gives us the word starboard.

It took courage to cross the ocean in a boat that was only 76 feet (23 metres) long. Waves could reach 100 feet (30 metres) and ship-wreck was common. There was little hope of being rescued by a passing ship.

Conditions were cramped and often cold, though each passenger had a leather sleeping bag for protection against the weather. They ate dried fish, salted meat, buttermilk and hard rye bread. Large casks held the water rations. The crew took it in turns to prepare the food, which could not be cooked because of the danger of fire.

A Viking widow, Auth the Deep-minded, emigrates to Iceland with her household. When land is sighted the high-seat pillars are thrown overboard. Wherever the pillars wash ashore will be the settlers' new home.

Things and Althings

Every freeman and freewoman could take part in the government of the country by attending the Thing (Assembly). Each district had its own Thing, which met every spring and autumn. The Things set taxes, made sure that every man had the correct weapons and investigated murders.

After about AD 902 Iceland had an Althing – Europe's earliest national assembly – which met each summer at the *Lögberg* (law rock) at Thingvellir, near present-day Reykjavik.

A *jarl* or *bóndi* who did not attend the Thing had to send a representative or pay a fine. However, widows and men who worked alone could stay at home, unless the Thing had been called on account of a murder or to choose a king.

A Thing lasted about a week. At the end, everybody showed their agreement with its decisions by clashing their weapons together. This was known as the *vápnatak* (weapon-shaking).

The Things had no power to enforce their decisions. Each Viking was bound only by a sense of duty to the community. Their community spirit, however, was very strong. The Icelanders were grouped together into *hreppr* (groups of about 20 farmers) which organized the sheep round-up, cared for the poor and compensated families who had the misfortune to lose their homes or crops. It was a Viking's duty to plough the old people's fields before he ploughed his own.

A *jarl* addresses a local Thing meeting. Although local government and legal matters are the main reasons for the Thing, people also come to trade, play games and exchange gossip.

Duel

If a Viking was murdered it was the duty
of the family – in particular the person who
performed *nábjargir* (see page 26) – to take
revenge. *Níth* (mockery) and insults could
also start a feud.

In the sagas it is usually the women who
insist on revenge. In *Njal's Saga* Hildigunn
throws her dead brother's cloak at her
husband Flosi, to goad him into avenging
his death. Flosi had wanted to ask the Thing
for compensation. 'This will finish us all,' he
warns her. He burns down Njal's house with
all the family inside. In his turn Njal's son-
in-law, Kari, kills Njal's murderers.

When two men were involved in this kind
of blood feud they often challenged each other
to a duel. Duels, however, could take place
for other reasons. They were a form of trial
by ordeal (see page 39) and a way of sorting
out quarrels. Sometimes a woman would
promise to marry the man who won her in
combat, leading to a fight to the death.

Berserkers sometimes made their living
from these contests, travelling the country
fighting for prizes. Many men, knowing they
could not win, simply handed over their
property or even their wives without a fight.

King Cnut of Denmark (996-1035) made
duelling and berserker behaviour illegal.

A *hólmganga* duel has strict rules. It is fought on a
cloak 10 feet (3 metres) square. If either man steps off
the cloak he is *nithing* (a coward).

The referee watches closely. Each man is allowed
three shields. If either man is wounded and his blood
falls on the cloak, he may withdraw. At the end the man
with most wounds pays his opponent in silver. If he
dies, all his property goes to the winner, so *hólmganga*
duels are usually fought to the death.

Viking Law

In the days before books the Vikings elected a law speaker to shout out their laws at each Althing.

Women's rights were protected. A girl who had reached the age of 15 could choose her own husband. A man could not kiss a woman who was not his wife, or even sing love songs to her. If he beat his wife, or wore his shirt open to show his chest, it was a disgrace and grounds for divorce.

In Sweden any crime, including murder, committed by a child below the age of 15 was said to be an accident.

If an adult was accused of a major crime by ten people, he or she went before the *lögrétta* (law court) on the Sunday of the Thing meeting. The *lögrétta* comprised the law speaker and 48 *gothis* (priests), each of whom had two advisers. The court was not a jury. It did not decide

whether a person was guilty or innocent, but simply announced what the law said.

There were no prisons. Criminals usually had to pay a fine, plus the doctor's bill if the crime involved injury. The fine for man-slaughter was called wergild (man value) and was paid to the family of the deceased. Small-time thieves were shaved and tarred and made to run the gauntlet (between two rows of people, who stoned them).

For the worst crimes, such as murdering a man during a truce, the criminal was out-lawed and could be killed at will.

The accused is brought before a panel of neighbours and given the chance to prove his innocence. He might swear by the gods on a priest's ring, or call 12 men to swear to his innocence. Alternatively, he might under-take an ordeal, such as walking over red-hot iron. An accused woman would pick holy stones from a cauldron of boiling water. Where one man accuses another, they might fight a duel. The Vikings believe that the gods will keep the innocent person safe.

Vinland

In 986 Eric the Red, a Norwegian living in Iceland, led an expedition of 25 ships across the Atlantic Ocean to Greenland. Fourteen of the ships arrived safely and a colony was established. Later on, according to the sagas, a Viking sailor called Bjarni was blown off course by a storm and sighted land still further west. In about AD 1000 Leif the Lucky, Eric the Red's son, retraced Bjarni's course and discovered a fertile country which he called Vinland.

The Greenlanders mounted two expeditions to colonize this new world. They built a village and traded with the natives (American Indians). However, these Skrælings, as they called them, soon began to attack the settlers. Thorvald, the leader of the first expedition, was killed by a Skræling arrow. On another occasion the small colony was saved from destruction only when one of the five women, who was a berserker, tore off her shirt, rushed at the attacking Skrælings and beat them over the head with the flat side of a sword until they fled.

Under the pressure of continual attack, and quarrels amongst themselves over the women, the colonists were forced to return to Greenland. In 1121 a Christian missionary set out to try to convert the Skrælings but was never seen again. Occasionally a ship from Greenland would carry to Norway strange furs of animals which at that time were found only in North America.

Viking colonists offer the Skrælings red cloth and milk in return for furs and skins.

Down the Dnieper

At the beginning of the ninth century Swedish and Danish traders sailed up-river into the centre of what is now called Russia. The local people called these travellers the Rus, from the Old Norse word for route.

The Rus conquered several cities, including Kiev, Novgorod and Smolensk, and used them as bases for raids and trading. There was an annual fair at Novgorod to which merchants came from all over Scandinavia. The Rus travelled on camels towards India and China to buy silk and lizard skins. They rode north to a land called Visu (possibly Siberia), where the days were only one hour long and the people were too shy to meet them face to face. The Vikings laid down their wares and left. When they returned they found furs beside their goods. They could keep the furs or take their own goods back.

Ibn Fadlan, a Muslim diplomat, met some of the Rus in 922. They were, he wrote, 'as tall as date palms', red-haired, light-skinned and covered with tattoos 'from the tips of their fingers to their necks'. He was fascinated and horrified. 'They are the filthiest of God's creatures,' he reported. In the morning a Rus slave would take a bowl of water to her master. He washed his hair, spat and blew his nose into it. Then each member of the household repeated the process, using the same bowl of water.

Some Russian historians do not believe that the Rus founded Russia, but it is clear that Scandinavians settled there. In Smolensk archaeologists have excavated a cemetery containing nearly 4,000 Swedish graves.

Rus traders carry their boat overland to avoid one of the seven sets of rapids on the River Dnieper in Russia. They slot the oars through the oar-holes and use them to lift the boat.

Trading Slaves

The Rus had no farmland, so they lived on what they could take as tribute from the local Slav tribes. During the winter they took furs and kidnapped men and women to sell as slaves. In summer they made the 1,500 mile (2,400 kilometre) journey towards Byzantium (Istanbul), selling their booty along the way.

The Vikings moored their boats near the marketplaces and built large warehouses. Each trader would set up a wooden post decorated with the image of a human face. He offered bread, meat and leeks to his idol. 'Please send me a merchant with lots of money,' he prayed, 'who will buy from me without too much haggling.'

Slave traders were said to be the richest of all merchants. A wealthy trader could offer his customers a choice of a dozen slaves. Sometimes he might have English monks and

other men and women kidnapped on raids in Europe, but mostly they were Slav peasants (the word slave comes from Slav).

A young boy might be exchanged for a goat or a fine rain-cloak. A female slave would cost a mark (200 grams of silver). A Viking called Höskuld paid three marks for a girl of 15 who was 'beautiful of face'. Later, she told him she was an Irish princess.

The Church tried to stop the slave trade because it did not like the idea of Christians being owned by Muslims. Once, when Bishop Rimbert of Denmark was riding past a line of slaves, one of the women shouted to him that she was a nun and sang psalms to prove it. The bishop immediately bought her from the merchant, although it cost him his horse and saddle and he had to walk back home.

A priest and a slave trader haggle over the price of four Christians who have been kidnapped and enslaved. The trader weighs the buyer's silver on his scales and tries to persuade him to pay more.

Miklagard

Rurik, a Viking ruler, and his son Igor, established a state in Russia during the ninth and tenth centuries. Some raiders continued down the rivers to the Caspian Sea where they were slaughtered by Muslim Arabs. Others sailed to the Black Sea and attacked Byzantium, which they called Miklagard (meaning 'the great city'). Although they were defeated, they were allowed to trade in Byzantium. Groups of no more than 50 could enter the city, provided they were not armed. In 957 Princess Olga, Igor's widow, visited the city and was received with great honour by the Emperor.

Between 980 and 1070 many Viking warriors fought as mercenaries in the personal bodyguard of the Emperor of Byzantium. They were called the Varangian Guard. The most famous man to join the Guard was Harald Hardrada (1015-66), often called 'the last Viking'. According to the sagas, he performed so many brave deeds during his time in the Guard that the Empress tried to stop him leaving. Harald's ship was trapped in Byzantium by an iron chain stretched across the harbour mouth. He ordered his men to stand in the back of the boat while he sailed it up onto the chain. Then he made them all run to the prow. The boat tipped forward, slid over the chain and escaped.

Pestered by traders, Varangian guards stand side by side with Byzantine soldiers as they guard the walls of Byzantium. They are proud of their unquestioning loyalty to the Emperor.

Battle at Sea

At about the time that the Varangian Guard was formed in Byzantium, a band of mercenaries called the Jomsvikings was formed in Denmark. Their fortress at Jomsborg, which had a harbour big enough for three hundred longships, is often mentioned in the sagas but has never been discovered.

The Jomsvikings had strict rules. Recruits had to be between 18 and 50, and unmarried. They had to avenge their fallen comrades and never flee from battle, whatever the circumstances. In one story a Jomsviking continued shooting his arrows even though both his feet had been cut off in the battle.

Jomsviking warriors fought in the two greatest naval battles of the Viking age: the Battle of Hjörungavag in 990, when King Svein Forkbeard of Denmark invaded Norway, and the Battle of Svold in 1000, when King Olaf

Tryggvason of Norway was ambushed by the kings of Sweden and Denmark. Although the Jomsvikings were famous for their strength and bravery, in both battles they fought on the losing side.

Both sides have tied their ships together to make a floating platform. Sails lowered and standards raised, the two fleets have been pulled together with grappling irons, so that the two forces can fight as if the battle was on land.

The enemy warriors have boarded the ship and are fighting their way along, driving the men back room by room. The air is full of taunts, oaths and the sound of horns. The captain stands in the stern of his ship, where his bodyguard have formed a shield wall to protect him.

The most important part of the fighting is in the prow of the ship, where the bravest warriors and berserkers are always positioned.

Berserkers do not always prove useful in sea battles, however. Sometimes they become so enraged that they forget where they are and charge right off the edge of the ship into the sea.

At the Wharfside

Despite the impression given by the writers of the time, most Vikings were traders, not raiders. Some Vikings, it is true, were blood-thirsty warriors, but many more spent their entire lives working peacefully as craftsmen or merchants.

The Vikings imported luxury items such as glassware, Rhineland pottery, French wines, spices from the East, jewellery and German swords. Silk caps discovered in the Viking towns of York and Lincoln in the north of England probably all came from the same roll of cloth, imported from Byzantium by a Viking trader.

In return, the Vikings traded the many valuable natural products found in Scandin-avia. From Norway came soapstone, a soft

stone that could be carved into cooking pots, and whetstones for sharpening tools and weapons. High-quality iron ore was found in Sweden. In addition, Scandinavian amber, furs, antlers and walrus tusks were much in demand.

In 960, Hedeby in Denmark is a bustling port. It is a centre for trade in all kinds of merchandise including antlers, jewellery, weapons, skins – and slaves, captured during raids on settlements in Russia and western Europe. A Jewish geographer visiting the town reports that life is hard and the inhabitants are poor. They live mainly on fish, which is plentiful. The main social life of the town takes place on feast days, when people gather together to honour their gods. 'Never have I heard such terrible singers as these,' the geographer writes. 'It is like a dog howling – only worse.'

There are twice as many men as women living in Hedeby. Trading and craftwork are thought to be unsuitable occupations for women.

Hedeby

During the Viking age in Scandinavia, towns grew up and became trading and manufacturing centres. Villages, which had once grown only enough food for their own needs, now tried to produce a surplus to sell to the towns. By the year 1000 there were many more Vikings living in towns than on *bærs*.

Nevertheless, even Hedeby, the largest town, would seem small today. There are ten thousand graves from the 250 years of Viking occupation, so it can be estimated that Hedeby had a population of only about one thousand people. Other important towns were Birka in Sweden and Kaupang in Norway.

Hedeby is a planned town occupying a site of about 10 acres (4 hectares). The streets, which are laid out in a grid pattern, are covered with wooden planking to prevent them becoming muddy when it rains, and the stream running through the town has planked sides to stop it flooding.

Most houses are built of wattle and daub – willow twigs threaded in and out of posts. Other buildings are made of horizontal planks fastened onto wooden stakes, or rows of planks hammered vertically into the soil. The thralls and poor freemen live at the other end of town, in damp sunken pits covered with thatched roofs.

The houses belonging to craftsmen and merchants are about 50 x 20 feet (15 x 6 metres) and face endways onto the street. Before a house is built the owner uses a yardstick to measure the site three times. If the second and third measurements are greater than the first, he believes that the ground is lucky and that his wealth will increase.

Each house has a yard, a well, a cesspit for sewage and a midden heap for rubbish. In this dyer's yard there are racks on which the cloth he has dyed in his vat (centre) is hung to dry. While people go about their daily tasks, a craftsman (left) tries to attract interest in the knives he has made.

In the Workshop

In towns such as Hedeby there were many specialist craftsmen who made the everyday items that the Vikings needed.

Carpenters made spoons and bowls, chests and chairs, beds and tables. They also helped to build boats, houses and churches. Many surfaces were decorated with detailed and intricate carvings. A Viking carpenter would do everything himself, from felling the tree to polishing the finished product.

Bone-carvers fashioned ice skates, hairpins, coat toggles and whorls (the weights used in spinning). Antler-carvers made combs, and playing pieces for the board game *hnefatafl*.

In a Viking town there would also be soap-stone carvers, coopers (who made barrels), cloth-makers, tanners (leather-workers), glass-bead specialists, locksmiths, jewellers and many other craftsmen. Everything was made by hand, in small workshops behind the craftsmen's houses.

Coins were used in Viking times, but most trade was done by barter – exchanging goods for other goods. Where this was impossible, merchants used silver jewellery as currency.

While a customer buys a necklace, the craftsman starts to hammer out a silver bracelet on an iron shoe inserted in a tree stump. Left, top to bottom: a Viking necklace, a brooch and a decorated axe-head.

The Coming of Christianity

Louis the Pious, the Holy Roman Emperor, sent a missionary to Scandinavia in AD 830 to convert the Vikings to Christianity. He hoped that if they became Christian they would stop raiding monasteries in Europe. The missionary, however, was attacked before he even set foot on land.

The Roman Catholic Church forbade Christians to trade with heathens, so Viking traders sometimes let themselves be prime-signed (given a cross to show their 'interest' in Christianity). Meanwhile, most Vikings continued to worship the old gods and became Christian only when forced by their kings to change their religion.

Olaf Tryggvason, King of Norway from 995 to 1000, introduced Christianity into Norway, Greenland and the Orkney Islands. In the year 1000 he demanded that Iceland,

too, should accept the new faith. After a fierce debate at the Althing, Thorgeir, the law speaker, suggested a compromise: Christianity would be the public religion, but people could make sacrifices to the Viking gods in private. Everyone agreed. A few years later the right to worship the old gods was removed.

Tryggvason's methods were not always so peaceful. Sometimes, accompanied by his soldiers, he broke into temples and smashed the idols. Even the names of some of his men – Bersi the Strong, Thrand the Squinting, Ketil the Tall, Eyvind Snake, Sigurd Axe, Grjotgard the Nimble, Orm Hoodnose – make them seem more like gangsters than missionaries.

Norwegian Vikings who resist conversion are tortured until they agree to accept Christianity. When Rauth, their leader, refuses to be converted, the king promises him a hideous death. A snake is placed in a hollow stick which will be forced between his teeth. The snake will slide down into his stomach and eat its way out of his side, killing him slowly and painfully.

Times of Change

Olaf Haraldsson, King of Norway from 1015 to 1030, continued Tryggvason's work. At Things all over the country the Norwegians were forced to accept Christianity. Olaf burned whole districts if the inhabitants opposed him. He put out the eyes of a nobleman called Hrærek, and cut off the tongue of the ruler of Dalir (a district in Norway) when he refused to be baptized. Those who accepted Christianity had to hand over their sons as hostages and as pledges of their faith.

Olaf's methods were so dreadful that eventually the Norwegians revolted against him. They drove him out of the country with the help of the Danes.

Something more than the spread of a religion was happening in Scandinavia. The kings who bullied their subjects into accepting Christianity were at the same time taking the opportunity to increase their own power. Baptism was often accompanied by a ceremony in which the person promised to become 'the king's man'. The influence of the Things declined; the power of the central government grew.

Sweden was the last Viking country to 'modernize' in this way. In about 994 Olaf Skottkonung, a Christian, became the first king of the whole of Sweden and began to convert the people. Paganism survived many years; as late as 1070 there was a great heathen revival led by Sacrifice Sven. In 1100, however, pagan worship was forbidden in Sweden and the old temples were destroyed.

Olaf Haraldsson, trying to regain power in Norway, is defeated and killed at the Battle of Stiklastad (1030). Although Olaf loses his life he gains immortality. Miracles are said to have been performed in his name and he is made a saint by the Roman Catholic Church.

The Viking Achievement

The Vikings were never united under one leader, yet they travelled, fought and traded in four continents. Their world extended from America to Siberia and from the Arctic to the Mediterranean. Harald Hardrada, who became King of Norway, fought in Russia, Byzantium, Scandinavia and England. He was a man of international stature. Gudrid, the wife of one of the first settlers in America, also went on a pilgrimage to Rome. She was the most widely travelled woman of her time.

It is strange to think, in this age of the superpowers, that at one time Vikings stood on the soil of both North America and Russia. Many of the Viking ideals – honour, law, democracy, the equality of women and the freedom of the individual – are still thought to be worth dying for a thousand years later.

Gradually, the power of the Vikings declined. In 1066, at the Battle of Stamford Bridge, Harald Hardrada was killed trying to conquer England. Hedeby was destroyed by tribesmen from Poland in the same year. In Russia the Rus married into the local population and lost contact with their Scandinavian relatives. Vinland was abandoned and forgotten. In Greenland the difficulties increased as the climate became colder. By 1410 the settlers had lost contact with Scandinavia and the colony slowly died out.

In Europe many states adopted the feudal system, giving local lords wealth and property in return for their services as cavalry soldiers in the army. The Vikings were no match for these heavily equipped, trained soldiers.

It is 1066. A Norman knight surveys the land given to him after the conquest of England. The Normans are the direct descendants of the Vikings who were granted Normandy by King Charles of France in 911.

How Do We Know?

One way of finding out about the Vikings is to read the books written by the people they attacked. The early raids on France and Germany were described in *The Frankish Annals* by French monks who witnessed the events. *The Anglo-Saxon Chronicle* is a year by year account of the history of England during these times and the Viking armies are frequently mentioned. However, it is necessary to remember that the French and the English were the Vikings' enemies and the monks who wrote the books were extremely biased.

Many people, such as the Muslim writer Ibn Fadlan, actually met and described the Vikings. The Emperor of Byzantium described the Rus in *The Book of Ceremonies*. He was giving advice to his son, so we can assume that he was telling the truth, but both he and Ibn Fadlan were describing Vikings whose customs had been changed by living in Russia.

The Deeds of the Archbishops of Hamburg, written by Adam of Bremen in about 1070, includes descriptions of the Vikings in Scandinavia. However, Adam of Bremen had never visited the countries he described; he merely reported what others had told him.

Other writings from the time are even less reliable. *The Nestor Chronicle* tells the early history of Russia, but it is clear that many of its stories are exaggerated. In one story the Vikings put wheels on their boats and sail them overland!

The sagas

The Vikings passed on their laws, religion, customs and history by word of mouth. Nothing was written down until about 1200, when their descendants began to record these things in books.

The most famous Norse stories are *Egil's Saga*, *Njal's Saga* and *The Saga of Olaf Tryggvason*, but there are dozens of others. Many were collected together during the 1220s by an Icelander called Snorri Sturluson. His book is called *The Heimskringla*.

The sagas are stories about real people; they are not legends. However, they are very biased in favour of the Vikings. In addition, there had been four hundred years for exaggerations and mistakes to creep in.

It is difficult to decide what to believe in the sagas. In *The Saga of Harald Hardrada*, for instance, Harald tricks a city into opening its gates by pretending that he wanted to bury one of his men. This story is similar to one told about a Viking leader called Hastings, who lived about two hundred years before Harald. Does this mean that the writer of Harald's saga heard the story and decided to use it to make Harald look good? Or maybe Harald had heard the story and tried the same ruse. It is even possible that both men really did think up the same clever trick to defeat their enemies, but we will never know the truth.

Other sources

A few of the Vikings' achievements have survived the centuries intact. Large defensive mounds such as the Danevirke, built by the Viking kings of Denmark, still exist. Some twelfth-century wooden churches can still be seen in Sweden. Rune stones, found all over Scandinavia, reveal a mass of small facts about the Vikings. Place names of Scandinavian origin show where the Vikings settled.

Archaeologists have dug up many other remains from Viking times. Some finds, such as the Swedish treasure hoards and the Gokstad ship, have been very exciting. Graves, especially those containing possessions, can

reveal a great deal about the lives and beliefs of the occupants.

Other excavations, such as Hedeby (now in Germany) and Jorvik (York) in England, have provided us with information about the lives of ordinary people. A Viking's diet, for instance, can be discovered from a piece of human excrement, and the scratches on the bottom of a ship can show how it was used.

Finding the answers

Occasionally, archaeologists have been able to link their findings to the stories in the sagas.

The Saga of Eric the Red, for example, tells how Thorvald, the brother of Leif the Lucky, led an expedition to a country to the west of Greenland where he was killed by the Skrælings.

Some people believed that the Vikings had discovered America, but by itself the evidence in the sagas could never prove that Vinland was Newfoundland. *The Saga of Eric the Red* was not written until about 1225, long after the events it claimed to be reporting. A 'Viking' map showing North America was found in Germany, but turned out to have been drawn with ink which was only available in the twentieth century.

For many years historians suspected that the saga writers had made up the stories. Then archaeologists found an American Indian arrowhead (perhaps the one that killed Thorvald) on Gudrid's farm in Greenland. They also found Viking coffins made from larch and maple, which grew only in North America in Viking times. Finally, in the 1960s, an ancient settlement was unearthed in Newfoundland. Finds included a hall with banks of earth along the walls in typical Viking style, a soapstone spinning-whorl and an iron nail (the American Indians did not work metal at this time). It had been proved beyond doubt that the Vikings discovered America and settled there for a time.

Archaeology will never be able to supply all the answers. The Jomsvikings' fortress, for instance, has never been discovered. Is this because it never existed, or has it been obliterated by later building?

Maybe, one day, a team of archaeologists will discover the lost fortress of Jomsborg. Perhaps, with luck and hard work, you will be a member of that team.

Index